Sunday Talks for Kids Ages 4–7

Sunday Talks for Kids Ages 4–7

Linda Prince and Amy Orton

WALNUT SPRINGS PRESS

Walnut Springs Press, LLC
110 South 800 West
Brigham City, Utah 84302
http://walnutspringspress.blogspot.com

ISBN: 978-1-935217-45-9

Portions of this book previously published in *Short Talks for Kids* (Leatherwood Press, 2008)

Contents

How to Use This Book

This book is full of Primary talks with a wide variety of themes. You should be able to find a talk that corresponds to your child's assigned topic. Here are some tips for helping your child give the talk:

- Encourage your child to bear his or her testimony after reading the talk. Even at an early age, a child can learn that a shared testimony brings the Spirit to a meeting, and that a testimony is strengthened by bearing it.

- The number listed after each talk refers to a picture in the Gospel Art Book (GAB) that can be used as a visual aid for your child's talk. You can buy a copy of the Gospel Art Book at any Church distribution center, at store.lds.org, or at deseretbook.com. You can also download and print the pictures at lds.org (go to "Resources," then "Video, Audio, and Images," then "Images," then "Gospel Art" under "Image Categories"). Some talks also suggest an image that is found only at lds.org (look under "Resources," then "Video, Audio, and Images," then "Images," then the image category listed after the talk in this book).

- Help your child read and practice the talk prior to giving it, and help him or her understand the topic. Answer any questions your child may have concerning the topic. Giving a talk is an opportunity for your child to learn more about the gospel.

Good luck!

One

I Am a Child of God

The Spirit itself beareth witness with our spirit,
that we are the children of God.

Romans 8:16

My Heavenly Father

Heavenly Father is the Father of my spirit.

I am so thankful that I am His child.

I am so thankful to know that He loves me.

He sent His Son to be the Savior because He loves me.

Heavenly Father has a plan to help me be happy.

Heavenly Father wants me to return to live with Him again.

He gave me a family because He loves me.

I am so grateful to know that I am a beloved child of Heavenly Father.

Visual Aid: GAB 112—Family Prayer

I Am a Child of God

I am a child of God, who loves me.

I lived with Him before I came to earth.

He created me in His image—

That means I look like Him!

I will keep all the commandments.

I will do what my parents ask me to do.

I will be kind to all of Heavenly Father's children.

Then I can live with Him and Jesus Christ someday.

Visual Aid: GAB 111—Young Boy Praying

Heavenly Father Loves and Blesses Me

I am thankful that I am a child of God.

I know Heavenly Father loves me.

He has blessed me with a body that works.

He has blessed me with a loving family.

He has blessed me with the gospel.

He has blessed me with prayer, so I can talk to Him every day.

He has blessed me with the scriptures and the prophet.

I am thankful I am a child of God and that He loves me.

Visual Aid: GAB 112—Family Prayer

Two

My Savior Jesus Christ

Hearken ye to these words. Behold, I am Jesus Christ, the Savior of the world. Treasure these things up in your hearts, and let the solemnities of eternity rest upon your minds.

Doctrine and Covenants 43:34

Jesus Christ Is My Savior

Jesus Christ is my Savior.

He is the Savior of every person on the earth.

He suffered for our sins in the Garden of Gethsemane.

He died for us on the cross.

After He died, He was resurrected.

Then He appeared to many people in the Holy Land.

He also went to the Americas to teach the Nephites who were righteous.

I am glad that Jesus Christ is my Savior.

Visual Aid: GAB 116—Christ and Children from around the World

The Birth of Jesus Christ

When Jesus was born, a bright new star shone in the sky.

The star was above the stable where He was born.

Shepherds came to see the baby Jesus as He lay in a manger.

Righteous people rejoiced when they heard about Jesus' birth.

Wise men from far away followed the new star.

It took them two years to find Jesus.

The wise men gave Him very special gifts, like gold.

The prophets' words were fulfilled when Jesus was born.

Visual Aid: GAB 31—The Angel Appears to the Shepherds

The Atonement and Resurrection of Jesus Christ

Jesus Christ did some very important things for me that I can't do for myself.

He took my sins upon Himself and felt pain for them.

Because of this, I can be forgiven if I repent.

Jesus laid down His life for me and was resurrected.

He did this so that after I die I can live again.

Jesus did all this for me because He loves me.

I love Him and I'm glad He is my Savior.

Visual Aid: GAB 59—Mary and the Resurrected Jesus Christ

Jesus Christ Is My Example

Jesus Christ is the perfect example.

He showed me how to do Heavenly Father's will.

Jesus was born on earth and grew up like I did,

But He always obeyed all of Heavenly Father's commandments.

Jesus did not question what His Father asked Him to do.

He knew Heavenly Father would only ask Him to do good things.

I will follow Jesus by always trying to do God's will.

Visual Aid: GAB 35—John the Baptist Baptizing Jesus

Three

Faith

*Faith is things which are hoped for and
not seen; wherefore, dispute not because ye
see not, for ye receive no witness until
after the trial of your faith.*

Ether 12:6

What Is Faith?

Faith is believing in things I can't see.

I know the wind blows, even though I can't see it.

I know the sun will come up every morning.

And I know that Heavenly Father and Jesus Christ love me.

I can't see them, but I know They are there.

The Holy Ghost will help me follow them.

Faith helps me to be happy and serve others.

I am happy that Heavenly Father has blessed me to have faith.

Visual Aid: GAK 65—Jesus at the Door

Faith in Jesus Christ

I have faith in Jesus Christ.

This means that I love him.

It means I believe in His words.

It means I know He is there for me.

It means I always try to do the things He has commanded me to do.

Because I have faith in Christ, I know He wants the best for me.

He wants me to be happy, and He knows the way.

I am so glad to know that Jesus Christ is my Savior.

Visual Aid: GAK 64—Jesus Carrying a Lost Lamb

Increasing My Faith

My faith in Jesus Christ grows every day.

I can gain more faith as I pray and read the scriptures.

I can gain more faith as my parents teach me about Jesus.

I can gain more faith as I take the sacrament.

I can gain more faith as I listen to the lessons in Primary.

Because I love Jesus Christ, I want to have more faith in Him.

I can follow Jesus every day.

Visual Aid: GAK 116—Christ and Children from around the World

Four

Prayer

Be thou humble; and the Lord thy God
shall lead thee by the hand,
and give thee answer to thy prayers.

Doctrine and Covenants 112:10

I Love to Pray

I love to talk to my Heavenly Father in prayer.

When I pray, I thank Him for His blessings.

I ask Him to help me to do what is right.

I ask Him to bless my family and friends and neighbors.

I ask Him to bless the prophet.

I ask Him to bless all the people in the world.

I also ask Him any questions I have.

Then I listen for His answers.

I am so glad I can pray to my Heavenly Father.

Visual Aid: GAB 111—Young Boy Praying

Heavenly Father Hears and Answers My Prayers

Heavenly Father commands us to pray to Him in Jesus' name.

Every day, I pray to Heavenly Father with my family.

I also pray by myself every day.

I can pray anywhere and anytime.

Heavenly Father will hear and answer my prayers.

Sometimes the answer will be no.

Sometimes it will be yes.

I am so happy I can pray to Heavenly Father.

Visual Aid: GAB 111– Young Boy Praying

Prayer in the Book of Mormon

Alma is a prophet in the Book of Mormon.

One day, the people he baptized were captured by Amulon, a wicked man.

Amulon placed guards over Alma's people and told them not to pray.

But they needed Heavenly Father's help and comfort,

So they prayed in their hearts instead of praying out loud.

The guards couldn't hear them, but Heavenly Father could.

He answered their prayers and helped them.

I can pray anywhere at any time, and He will help me, too.

Visual Aid: GAB 76—Alma Baptizes in the Waters of Mormon

Five

Baptism and Confirmation

Come unto me, and be baptized in my name,
that ye may receive a remission of your sins,
and be filled with the Holy Ghost.

3 Nephi 30:2

Baptism Is Important

Baptism is very important.

When a person is baptized, he or she stands in the water.

A priesthood holder stands in the water too.

He says a special prayer.

Then he places the person being baptized under the water for a moment.

The water washes away the person's sins.

Jesus wants everyone to be baptized into His Church.

That is because He wants us to return to live with Him and Heavenly Father.

I am excited to be baptized when I am eight years old.

Visual Aid: GAB 104—Girl Being Baptized

I Will Be Baptized

When I turn eight years old, I will be baptized.

I will do this to show my love for Heavenly Father.

I will do this to obey His commandments.

I will be baptized to get on the path to return to Him.

My dad or another priesthood holder will baptize me.

All my sins will be washed away.

After I am baptized, I will be confirmed a member of Christ's Church.

And I will receive the gift of the Holy Ghost.

I will show my faith in Jesus Christ by being baptized and confirmed.

Visual Aid: GAB 104—Girl Being Baptized

I Will Be Confirmed

After I am baptized, I will be confirmed a member of the Church and receive the gift of the Holy Ghost.

He will help me make good choices.

He will guide and protect me throughout my life.

He will help me understand the scriptures and the things I am taught in Primary.

When I get sad, the Holy Ghost will help me to be happy again.

I am excited to receive the gift of the Holy Ghost.

I can't wait to turn eight so I can be baptized and confirmed.

Visual Aid: GAB 105—The Gift of the Holy Ghost

Six

The Holy Ghost

God shall give unto you knowledge
by his Holy Spirit, yea, by the unspeakable
gift of the Holy Ghost.
Doctrine and Covenants 121:6

The Holy Ghost

The Holy Ghost is the third member of the Godhead.

The Holy Ghost is the Spirit of God.

He is sometimes called the Holy Spirit or just the Spirit.

Heavenly Father speaks to His children through the Holy Ghost.

The Holy Ghost testifies of Heavenly Father and Jesus Christ.

The Holy Ghost gives me answers and feelings in my mind and heart.

I am happy when I listen to Him.

After I am baptized, I will be confirmed and receive the gift of the Holy Ghost.

Visual Aid: GAB 105—The Gift of the Holy Ghost

The Holy Ghost Guides Me

The Holy Ghost usually speaks with a still small voice.

The Holy Ghost will help me make good choices.

He will warn me of danger.

He will help me to feel sad when I have done something wrong.

He will help me to obey my parents.

He will help me to be kind to others.

He will help me to understand the scriptures.

I am thankful for the gift of the Holy Ghost.

Visual Aid: GAB 105—The Gift of the Holy Ghost

The Gift of the Holy Ghost

When I am eight, I will receive the gift of the Holy Ghost.

The Holy Ghost can bless me in many ways.

He will speak to me in my heart and my mind.

He will prompt me to repent.

He will help me to always live righteously.

He will help me to be happy and to serve others.

I will have the Holy Ghost with me all the time after I am confirmed.

I am grateful for the gift of the Holy Ghost.

Visual Aid: GAB 105—The Gift of the Holy Ghost

Seven

Repentance and Forgiveness

Yea, and as often as my people repent will I forgive them their trespasses against me.

Mosiah 26:30

I Can Repent

When I do something bad, I can repent.

Maybe I have been unkind to one of my friends.

I can repent by praying and asking Heavenly Father to forgive me,

And by asking my friend to forgive me.

Then I try not to do the bad thing again.

I can repent because Jesus Christ suffered for my sins.

I need to repent so I can return to Heavenly Father.

I am happy that I can repent and learn to be a better person.

Visual Aid: GAB 56—Jesus Praying in Gethsemane

The Savior's Atonement

Jesus Christ knew I would sin.

He knew this would mean I could not live with Heavenly Father again.

So Jesus suffered for my sins.

This is called the Atonement.

Because of it, I can be forgiven of my sins if I repent.

I will remember what Jesus did for me.

I will try to choose the right, but when I make mistakes I will repent.

Then I can return to live with Heavenly Father and Jesus someday.

Visual Aid: GAB 56—Jesus Praying in Gethsemane

Loving and Forgiving Others

When someone does something mean to me, I have two choices.

I can get angry and act mean back.

Or I can forgive the other person.

To forgive means to not be angry because of what someone else did.

To forgive means to be kind to people even if they make mistakes.

To forgive means to love others.

Jesus Christ teaches us that we should forgive people.

I will follow His teachings and forgive others.

Visual Aid: GAB 56—Jesus Praying in Gethsemane

Jesus Taught Me to Forgive

When Jesus Christ was hanging on the cross, He forgave the soldiers who put Him there.

He asked Heavenly Father to forgive them too.

Jesus wasn't angry at the soldiers for following the orders they were given.

He knew they didn't realize they were doing something wrong.

He knew they didn't realize He was the Son of God.

The prophet teaches us to be like Jesus.

The prophet teaches us to forgive.

I can forgive others like Jesus did.

Visual Aid: GAB 57—The Crucifixion

Eight

Family

The family is ordained of God.

"The Family: A Proclamation to the World," paragraph 7

Heavenly Father Sent Me to a Family

Heavenly Father sent me to my family.

He knew they would love me.

He knew they would help me learn and grow.

He also knew I could help my family be more like Jesus.

I will do this by obeying my parents.

I will do this by being kind to my brothers and sisters.

I will do this by having faith.

I will do this by being an example.

I am grateful that Heavenly Father sent me to my family.

Visual Aid: GAB 112—Family Prayer

I Will Obey My Parents

The Lord has commanded us to obey our parents.

He said, "Thou shalt honor thy father and thy mother."

The Book of Mormon has many examples of this.

Nephi obeyed his father and went to get the brass plates.

Enos remembered his father's words and prayed for forgiveness.

The stripling Lamanite warriors listened to their mothers and were protected.

I will obey my mom and dad.

I know they will teach me what is right.

I am thankful for my parents.

Visual Aid: GAB 70—Nephi Subdues His Rebellious Brothers

Families Are Important

Families are an important part of Heavenly Father's plan.

My dad uses the priesthood to bless our family.

My mother makes me feel special and loved.

My brother and sisters play with me.

My grandparents tell me stories.

My aunts and uncles like to spend time with me.

I have fun with my cousins.

I love all the members of my family.

I am grateful Heavenly Father sent me to them.

(Change wording according to child's family situation.)

Visual Aid: GAB 112—Family Prayer

Families Are Forever

My Mommy and Daddy got married in the temple.

This means I can be with my family forever if I am good and follow Jesus.

I will honor my parents and be kind to my brothers and sisters.

I will keep the commandments.

I will pray to Heavenly Father in the name of Jesus Christ.

I will be baptized and confirmed when I am eight years old.

I will repent when I do something wrong

I want to live with my family and Jesus forever.

(Change wording according to child's family situation.)

Visual Aid: GAB 120—Young Couple Going to the Temple

Nine

Serving God and Others

Thou shalt love the Lord thy God with all thy heart, with all thy might, mind, and strength; and in the name of Jesus Christ thou shalt serve him.

Doctrine and Covenants 59:5

I Will Serve God

I am a child of God, who loves me very much.

He has commanded me to serve Him.

I will serve Him by having faith.

I will serve Him by keeping the commandments.

I will serve Him by helping others.

I will serve Him by sharing my testimony.

Because I am Heavenly Father's child,

I will serve Him with all my heart, might, mind, and strength.

Visual Aid: GAB 111—Young Boy Praying

I Love to Serve Heavenly Father

I love to serve Heavenly Father.

I do this by praying to Him morning and night.

I serve Him by helping my family to remember to pray together.

I serve Heavenly Father by doing what He asks me to do.

I serve Him by being reverent.

I serve Him by paying my tithing.

I serve Him by sharing the gospel with others.

I serve Him by being kind to others.

Heavenly Father blesses me so much, and I love to serve Him.

Visual Aid: GAB 113—Payment of Tithing

Showing Love for Heavenly Father

I want to show Heavenly Father that I love Him.

So I will show respect and kindness to everyone.

I will be friendly and say hello to people I know.

When someone needs help, I will lend a hand.

When I notice that someone feels bad,

I will ask if they are okay and try to cheer them up.

I will try to be kind even when someone is unkind to me.

I will show Heavenly Father that I love all His children too.

Visual Aid: GAB 115—Service

Serving God by Serving Others

King Benjamin is a prophet in the Book of Mormon.

He taught the commandments to his people.

He told them that as they served others, they were also serving God.

I can serve others by loving them and helping them.

When I serve others, I am happy.

It makes Heavenly Father happy, too.

I love Him and want to serve Him.

I will serve Him by helping my friends and family.

Visual Aid: GAB 74—King Benjamin Addresses His People

Ten

Following the Prophet

Surely the Lord God will do nothing, but he revealeth his secret unto his servants the prophets.

Amos 3:7

Our Prophet Serves Us

Our prophet is the President of the Church.

He serves us in many ways.

He tells us what the Lord wants us to hear.

The prophet travels all around the world to teach people about the gospel.

He spends most of his time serving the Church.

He loves all of the people in the world, not just Church members.

He serves us because he loves us.

He serves us because he loves Heavenly Father.

I am glad we have a prophet to show us the way.

Visual Aid: GAB 137—Thomas S. Monson (or download image titled "President Thomas S. Monson, President of the Church," at lds.org, under image category "Church Leadership")

Prophets and Apostles

In our Church, we have prophets and apostles.

The Quorum of the Twelve has twelve apostles, just like in Jesus' day.

The First Presidency has three apostles.

The President of the Church is the senior apostle and is called "the prophet."

Jesus directs the Church through the prophet.

The other apostles also help direct the Church.

All of the apostles teach us what the Lord wants us to do.

I am grateful we have prophets and apostles.

Visual Aid: GAB 137—Thomas S. Monson (or download image "President Thomas S. Monson, President of the Church," or "Quorum of the Twelve Apostles," at lds.org, under image category "Church Leadership")

Following the Prophet

Heavenly Father and Jesus Christ give the prophet important messages.

The prophet gives those messages to us.

He teaches us to keep the commandments.

He warns us of things that are bad for us.

I know the prophet speaks the truth.

I know I will be happy if I do what he says.

The prophet will never lead me astray.

I will follow the prophet.

Visual Aid: GAB 137—Thomas S. Monson (or download image "President Thomas S. Monson, President of the Church," at lds.org, under image category "Church Leadership")

The Prophet's Teachings

Heavenly Father gives us prophets.

The prophet teaches us how to return to Heavenly Father someday.

The prophet teaches us to be kind to others.

He teaches us to pay our tithing.

He teaches us to obey the commandments.

The prophet teaches us to be baptized.

He teaches us to be married in the temple.

If we do these things, we can live with Heavenly Father again.

I am glad He gave us a prophet.

Visual Aid: GAB 137—Thomas S. Monson (or download image "President Thomas S. Monson, President of the Church," at lds.org, under image category "Church Leadership")

Eleven

Scriptures

Search the scriptures; for in them ye think ye have eternal life: and they are they which testify of me.

John 5:39

I Love the Scriptures

I love to read the scriptures to learn about Heavenly Father and Jesus Christ.

I learn that They showed Nephi how to build a ship to cross the ocean.

I learn that They told Moses to lead the Israelites out of bondage.

I learn that They helped Joseph Smith translate the gold plates.

I learn about Jesus blessing the children.

I learn about all of His miracles.

I learn how much He and Heavenly Father love me.

I grow closer to Them when I read the scriptures.

Visual Aid: GAB 73—Mormon Abridging the Plates

The Bible

The Bible is a book of scripture that is very old.

It says Jesus Christ is the Son of God.

Bible stories help me learn about the gospel.

From Daniel, I learn that Heavenly Father will protect me.

From Jonah, I learn to obey the commandments.

From Moses, I learn that the Lord can do miracles.

From Esther, I learn that the Lord watches over His people.

From Peter, I learn to have faith in Jesus.

From Paul, I learn to do missionary work.

From Jesus, I learn to trust in Heavenly Father.

I will read the Bible so I can learn how to live the gospel.

Visual Aid: GAB 89—Joseph Smith Seeks Wisdom in the Bible

The Book of Mormon

Book of Mormon stories teach me to keep the commandments.

Nephi shows me how to obey the Lord.

Mosiah teaches me to serve others.

Alma teaches me about missionary work.

He also teaches me about repentance.

Samuel teaches me to listen to the prophet.

Ether teaches me to have faith like the brother of Jared.

Moroni teaches me to pray to the Lord and ask for help.

I love to read the stories in the Book of Mormon.

They teach me how to live the gospel.

Visual Aid: GAB 86—Moroni Hides the Plates in the Hill Cumorah

The Doctrine and Covenants

The Doctrine and Covenants teaches me how to live the gospel.

This book contains Jesus' commandments to us in the latter days.

The Doctrine and Covenants is often called the D&C.

It teaches me to follow the prophets.

It gives us the sacrament prayers.

It teaches me to be a missionary.

It teaches me to keep the Sabbath day holy.

The D&C teaches me about eternal marriage.

The D&C teaches me how to have a healthy body.

I will read the D&C so I can learn to keep the commandments.

Visual Aid: GAB—Blessing the Sacrament

Twelve

Thanking God in All Things

He commanded them that . . . every day
they should give thanks to the Lord their God.

Mosiah 18:23

Giving Thanks to Heavenly Father

Heavenly Father gives us so many blessings.

We need to thank Him for them every day.

He has a plan for us so we can return to live with Him.

He created our spirits.

He created the earth through His Son Jesus Christ.

Heavenly Father let us come to earth and get a body.

He gives us our families.

He gives us prophets and priesthood and temples.

I will thank Heavenly Father for all of these blessings.

When I am thankful, I feel happy.

Visual Aid: GAB 112—Family Prayer

Being Grateful Every Day

Heavenly Father is so good to me and my family.

I want to thank Him every day.

He blesses us with food to eat.

He blesses us with clothes to wear.

He blesses us with a house to live in.

He blesses us with health and strength.

He blesses us with friends and neighbors.

He blesses us with chances to learn.

I am grateful for all of Heavenly Father's blessings

So I will be sure to thank Him every day.

Visual Aid: GAB 111—Young Boy Praying

I Will Give Thanks to God

God is the Father of my spirit.

He wants me to be happy and to live with Him again.

He wants me to be happy.

He gives me air to breathe.

He gives me a beautiful earth to live on.

He gives me a loving family.

He gives me the gospel and the true Church of Jesus Christ.

Heavenly Father only asks me to keep the commandments

And to thank Him for all that He gives me.

I will thank Him because I love Him.

I will thank Him because He loves me.

Visual Aid: GAB 111—Young Boy Praying

I Am Thankful for My Body

I am thankful to Heavenly Father for my body.

I will treat it like a temple and keep it clean.

I will dress modestly.

I will not smoke, drink, or use drugs.

I will eat good food and I will exercise.

I will go to bed on time so I can get enough sleep.

Then I will feel the Holy Ghost with me always,

Especially after I am baptized and confirmed.

It is part of Heavenly Father's plan for me to have a body.

I will take care of it and thank Him for it.

Visual Aid: GAB 104—Girl Being Baptized

Thirteen

Jesus Christ Restored His Church

And I have sent forth the fulness of my gospel
by the hand of my servant Joseph;
and in weakness have I blessed him.
Doctrine and Covenants 35:17

Jesus Christ Restored His Church

After Jesus died and was resurrected, He went back to heaven.

Once His twelve apostles died, people stopped believing in Jesus' gospel.

Because of this, the Church was taken away.

Hundreds of years later, Jesus Christ restored it.

He restored the fulness of His gospel.

He did this through the Prophet Joseph Smith.

Because we have the gospel and the true Church, we can be happy.

I am glad the Savior restored His Church.

Visual Aid: GAB 38—Christ Ordaining the Apostles

The First Vision

When Joseph Smith was fourteen years old,

He went to a grove of trees to pray.

He asked Heavenly Father which church he should join.

Heavenly Father and Jesus Christ appeared to Joseph.

They told him all the churches were wrong.

They said he shouldn't join any of them.

Joseph listened to Jesus and Heavenly Father.

Joseph became a prophet of God.

Jesus Christ restored His Church through Joseph Smith.

I am grateful we have the true Church.

Visual Aid: GAB 90—The First Vision

The Restoration

After Jesus Christ died, people stopped believing in Him.

So Heavenly Father took away the Church.

After hundreds of years, Jesus Christ restored the Church through Joseph Smith.

Because the Church was restored, we have the gospel.

We have the Book of Mormon.

We have the priesthood and prophets and temples.

We know we can return to our Heavenly Father and our Savior Jesus Christ.

I am so happy I belong to the true Church.

Visual Aid: GAB 92—Joseph Smith Translating the Book of Mormon

Fourteen

Sharing the Gospel

Let your light so shine before men,
that they may see your good works,
and glorify your Father which is in heaven.
Matthew 5:16

Telling My Friends about the Gospel

Some of my friends do not belong to the Church.

They don't know all the wonderful things I know.

I want all my friends to be happy,

So I tell them about the gospel.

I like sharing my testimony.

I like talking about Jesus Christ and His teachings.

I like helping others.

I love serving my friends by teaching them gospel truths.

When I tell my friends about the gospel, it blesses their lives.

Visual Aid: GAB 115—Service

Being a Good Example

Other people notice what I do, so I try to do what is right.

When I am nice to my brother or sister, I help others remember to be nice.

When I choose not to drink or smoke or say bad words, I can teach other people not to do these bad things.

When I live the gospel standards, I teach other people about the gospel.

That is what Jesus did.

He was a good example to those around Him.

I can be a missionary now by choosing the right.

Visual Aid: GAB 109—Missionaries: Elders

I Will Share the Gospel

I know we are all children of God and that He loves us.

Some of my friends don't know about Heavenly Father.

So I will tell them about Him and Jesus Christ.

I will tell my friends about the commandments.

I will tell them about prophets and apostles.

I will tell them about temples and eternal families.

I will tell them I know the Church is true.

I will tell them the gospel makes me happy.

I love sharing it with others.

Visual Aid: GAB 110—Missionaries: Sisters

I Will Prepare to Be a Missionary

I can prepare to be a missionary by being faithful and obedient.

Missionaries teach people about the scriptures.

I can prepare for a mission by reading the scriptures every day.

Missionaries teach people to pray.

I can prepare for a mission by saying my prayers every day.

I can prepare for a mission by obeying Heavenly Father and my parents.

I can prepare for a mission by listening to the prophet.

I am excited to be a missionary someday.

Visual Aid: GAB 109—Missionaries: Elders

Fifteen

The Temple

Let this house be built unto my name,
that I may reveal mine ordinances
therein unto my people.

Doctrine and Covenants 124:40

The Temple Is a Gift from Heavenly Father

Heavenly Father has given us a special gift to help us return to Him.

It is the temple.

In the temple, we receive ordinances and make covenants with the Lord.

The temple is His house.

I want to go there someday so I can feel closer to Him

I want to receive the blessings He has in store for me.

I will prepare now to go to the temple.

I will choose the right and keep the commandments.

I am glad Heavenly Father has given us temples.

Visual Aid: GAB 119—Salt Lake Temple

Preparing to Go to the Temple

When I am older, I will go to the temple.

I need to prepare so that I am worthy to go.

I will prepare by obeying the commandments.

I will prepare by always following Jesus Christ.

I will prepare by being baptized and confirmed.

I will prepare by being reverent in church.

I will prepare by dressing modestly.

I will prepare by treating others kindly.

Preparing to go to the temple makes me happy.

Visual Aid: GAB 104—Girl Being Baptized

Temple Blessings

The temple is a beautiful place.

Someday, I will go there to receive special blessings.

I will also make promises, or covenants, to Heavenly Father there.

If my parents were not married in the temple before I was born,

I can go to the temple to be sealed to them if we are worthy.

After I go to the temple for myself, I will go for people who have died.

I will help them receive their temple blessings.

One day I will be married in the temple.

The temple is a wonderful gift from my Heavenly Father.

Visual Aid: GAB 120—Young Couple Going to the Temple

I Will Help My Ancestors

I am blessed to have the gospel in my life.

But some of my ancestors didn't know about the Church.

They died without being baptized.

After they died, they were taught the gospel.

But they can't be baptized and confirmed without my help.

They can't receive their temple ordinances without my help.

I can help my parents find my ancestors' names.

When I get older, I can help my ancestors receive their temple blessings.

Then they can live with Heavenly Father again.

Visual Aid: GAB 121—Temple Baptismal Font

Sixteen

The Creation

And there stood one among them that was like unto God, and he said unto those who were with him: We will go down, for there is space there, and we will take of these materials, and we will make an earth whereon these may dwell;

And we will prove them herewith, to see if they will do all things whatsoever the Lord their God shall command them.

Abraham 3:24–25

The Earth Is Part of Heavenly Father's Plan

Heavenly Father has a plan for His children.

It is called the plan of salvation or the plan of happiness.

Heavenly Father wants us to become like Him.

To do that, we needed a place where we could have a body.

We needed a place where we could learn to make right choices.

So Heavenly Father directed Jesus Christ to create the earth.

The earth is beautiful and special.

I am grateful that Jesus created it for us.

Visual Aid: GAB 3—The Earth

Jesus Christ Created the Earth

Jesus Christ created the world where we live.

In the Bible, we learn about each day of the Creation.

Jesus made the earth and separated the light from the darkness.

He separated the land from the water.

Then he put plants like trees and grass on the earth.

Next he put animals of all kinds on the earth.

He put fishes and other creatures in the water.

Last of all, Adam and Eve were created.

The earth is beautiful.

I am happy that I live on the earth.

Visual Aid: GAB 2—The Lord Created All Things

Adam and Eve

After the earth was created, Heavenly Father created Adam and Eve.

They were the first people on the earth.

They were our first parents.

For a while, they lived in the Garden of Eden.

Then they lived in the lone and dreary world.

Adam and Eve prayed to Heavenly Father and offered sacrifice.

He gave commandments to Adam and Eve.

Adam and Eve had many children and taught them the gospel.

I am grateful for Adam and Eve, our first parents.

Visual Aid: GAB 4—Adam and Eve Kneeling at an Altar

Seventeen

The Second Coming

I know that my redeemer liveth, and that he shall stand at the latter day upon the earth.

Job 19:25

Jesus Christ Will Come Again

A long time ago, Jesus Christ came to earth.

He was the Son of God but was born as a baby.

After He grew up, He died and was resurrected.

He will never die again.

One day, Jesus will come back to the earth.

Everybody will know that He has come.

It will be a happy day for the good people.

It will be a sad day for the bad people.

I am glad that Jesus will come back to the earth someday.

Visual Aid: GAB 66—The Second Coming

I Will Watch for the Second Coming

After Jesus Christ was resurrected, He visited His disciples.

Then He went to heaven to live with Heavenly Father.

Angels told the disciples that Jesus would come again.

We watch for that day, which we call the Second Coming.

Only Heavenly Father knows the day and the hour when Jesus will return.

Jesus will come to save His people and to set up His kingdom on the earth.

Then the whole world will be peaceful.

I am excited for Jesus to come again.

Visual Aid: GAB 62—The Ascension of Jesus

The Second Coming and the Millennium

Jesus Christ went to heaven after He was resurrected.

But He will come again in power and glory.

He will claim the earth as his kingdom.

After His Second Coming, there will be a thousand years of peace.

The thousand years of peace is called the Millennium.

Jesus will reign on earth.

Everyone will do what is right.

We will do temple work for others.

It will be wonderful when Jesus comes again.

Visual Aid: GAB 66—The Second Coming